MEAN MACHINES

MOTORBIKES

MARK MORRIS

Raintree

www.raintreepublishers.co.uk

Visit our website to find out more information about **Raintree** books.

To order:
 Phone 44 (0) 1865 888113
 Send a fax to 44 (0) 1865 314091
 Visit the Raintree Bookshop at **www.raintreepublishers.co.uk** to browse our catalogue and order online.

First published in Great Britain by Raintree,
Halley Court, Jordan Hill, Oxford OX2 8EJ,
part of Harcourt Education.
Raintree is a registered trademark of
Harcourt Education Ltd.

Editorial: Charlotte Guillain and Richard Woodham
Design: Michelle Lisseter and Bridge Creative
Services Ltd
Picture Research: Bea Ray and Pete Morris
Production: Jonathan Smith
Index: Indexing Specialists (UK) Ltd

Originated by Ambassador
Printed and bound in China by South China
Printing Company

ISBN 1 844 43163 0 (hardback)
08 07 06 05 04
10 9 8 7 6 5 4 3 2 1
ISBN 1 844 43168 1 (paperback)
09 08 07 06 05
10 9 8 7 6 5 4 3 2 1

British Library Cataloguing in Publication Data
Morris, Mark
Motorbikes – (Mean Machines)
1. Motorcycles – Juvenile Literature
I. title
629.2'275

A full catalogue record for this book is available from
the British Library.

Acknowledgements
Alamy p.**42**; Alvey and Towers pp. **14, 24, 33, 49, 52**;
Andrew Morland pp. **7, 10, 17, 18**; BMW p.**26**;
Car Photo Library pp. **25, 26, 28**; Corbis pp. **8, 9**
(Bettman), **20** (Roger Ressmeyer), **44** (top), **44** (bot)
(Bettman), **47** (Patrick Ward), **48** (Adam Woolfit), **50**
(Bettman), **57**; Dave Campos p.**5**; Dorling Kindersley
p.**11**; Ducati p.**6**; Empics pp. **31, 32, 34–35, 36, 37,
38, 40** (bot); Eye Ubiquitous p.**43** (Darren Maybury);
Giles Chapman pp. **54, 56**; Harley Davidson pp. **16**
(bot), **29** (bot); Honda pp. **16** (bot), **30, 46, 54**;
Mirrorpix pp. **4, 22, 22, 23, 35, 52, 55**; National
Motor Museum, Beaulieu pp. **8, 10, 45**;
PA Photos pp. **38, 39, 50**; Phoenix Distribution p.**21**;
Rex Features pp. **19, 51**; Ron Kimball Studios p.**53**;
Sporting Pictures p.**41**; Suzuki pp. **14, 15, 24, 37, 46**;
Sylvia Cordaiy p.**32–33**; Topfoto pp. **6, 12, 30, 34,
36, 40** (top), **42, 48, 56**; TRH Pictures pp. **12, 13, 29**;
Triumph Motorcycles pp. **20, 27**; Triumph p.**18–19**.

Cover photograph of a Kawasaki Ninja reproduced
with permission of Action Plus.

Every effort has been made to contact copyright
holders of any material reproduced in this book. Any
omissions will be rectified in subsequent printings if
notice is given to the publishers.

Disclaimer
All the Internet addresses (URLs) given in this book
were valid at the time of going to press. However, due
to the dynamic nature of the Internet, some addresses
may have changed, or sites may have changed or

CONTENTS

Any words appearing in the text in bold, **like this**, are explained in the Glossary. You can also look out for them in the Up To Speed box at the bottom of each page.

THE BEST BIKES

This book is not interested in ordinary motorbikes. It is only interested in the best: motorbikes that beat the rest.

The best bikes do things that others cannot. A racing motorbike can **accelerate** like a rocket and fly around corners at incredible speeds. An off-road motorbike can handle difficult conditions and jump over obstacles. Then there are **production motorbikes**. These are superbikes designed to **perform** like track racers, but any member of the public can buy one.

There are also the motorbikes that just want to go faster and faster. Some are specially built to break records. Others take part in dragster meetings.

CRUISER

Bikes like the Harley-Davidson Road King **cruiser** have an old-fashioned design. They are just as much about image and style as **performance**.

A Harley-Davidson FLHR Road King.

cruiser   motorbike built for comfort, looks and style
limited edition   when only a small number are built

TREMENDOUS TWO-WHEELERS

You can see great bikes on the streets and you can hear them, too! You could go to a race track to see professionals racing amazing machines to their limits.

There are lots of bike shows where you can see awesome motorbikes. There are competitions for the best bikes and sometimes there are display shows, too.

There are even fantastic bikes in museums, especially if they were a **limited edition** design or held a speed record.

Wherever you see them, one thing will stay the same. Motorbikes are exciting. You get a thrill just from looking at them.

This bike holds the land-speed record for motorbikes.

FIND OUT LATER...

Which bikes have races that are over in seconds?

How are bikes used by the army?

Which bike has a roof?

perform / performance   how well a bike does things
production motorbikes   bikes built in large numbers

THE MOTORBIKE STORY

There are different kinds of motorbike for different styles of riding. Touring bikes are designed to be comfortable on long journeys. Off-road bikes are designed for fun on dirt tracks. **Cruisers** are designed for low-speed travel around town.

Then there are the 'superbikes'. With superbikes, **performance** is the only thing that matters. They are built to be thrilling to ride. A superbike's weight, size and power are carefully balanced to give maximum performance and excitement.

INDIAN HENDEE SPECIAL

This 1914 Indian Hendee Special was the first bike to have an electric starter. It only cost US $325 to buy. Fewer than seven are still known to exist today.

TECH TALK

Ducati 998s: technical data
- Engine size: 998 cc
- Engine type: L twin **cylinder**
- Engine power: 123 **bhp**
- Top speed: 265.6 km/h (165 mph)
- Weight: 198 kg

cc (cubic centimetre)   this number measures the size of an engine's cylinders; a higher number means a larger engine

Riding a superbike means being out on the edge. They ride low to the ground and at very high speeds. They are the machines for speed freaks.

High-performance sports bikes are built to look like racing machines. They go so quickly thanks to a balance of weight and power. The lighter a bike is, the less engine power is needed to make it go. Lightweight bikes with very powerful engines can be difficult to control, however.

There are also many different sorts of racing competitions. Some races use specially built machines, others use **production motorbikes**.

SUZUKI RGV500

The Suzuki RGV500 has a 500 **cc** engine but weighs only 130 kg. That is about 30–40 kg lighter than most 500 cc bikes. As a result it has been a successful racing bike and can reach speeds of 296 km/h (185 mph).

A Suzuki RGV500.

cylinder   tube-shaped part of an engine, where fuel is burned
bhp   rate at which an engine does work

THE FIRST POWERED BIKES

The very first motorbikes were built in the mid-nineteenth century. They used steam engines to power them. These engines needed to burn wood or coal to make them go. Wood and coal are very heavy, and the engines took a long time to warm up. Steam-bikes belched out thick black smoke and had a nasty habit of exploding!

By the 1880s, petrol engines were being used to power bikes. They were much better because they were ready to ride as soon as the engine started.

The first motorbikes went on sale in the early 1900s. They were ordinary pedal bikes with small engines bolted on to them.

DAIMLER

In 1885, Gottlieb Daimler built one of the first coal-powered motorbikes. His son Paul rode it for 13 kilometres (8 miles) at a top speed of 16 km/h (10 mph). Unfortunately, Paul had to get off rather quickly when the bike burst into flames.

TECH TALK

The 1901 Werner was the first motorbike to have its engine in the place we expect to find it today.

reputation   being well known for something

EARLY MOTORBIKES

By 1914, proper motorbikes were being built. Rather than attaching tiny petrol engines to pedal bikes, companies could see that the motorbike had a future.

Motorbikes built by the company 'Indian' were very popular. George Hendee and Oscar Hedstrom started the company, which soon gained a **reputation** for good design and high quality.

Before long, many other companies were building motorbikes. They came in strange shapes and sizes. Slowly they began to look more like the sorts of machines we see on the roads today.

THE WORLD'S FIRST

The 1894 Hildebrand and Wolfmuller Motorrad was the world's first **production motorbike**. It was difficult to start and even harder to ride. But it was the first!

The 1894 Hildebrand and Wolfmuller had a top speed of 45 km/h (28 mph).

BETWEEN THE WARS

The 1920s were the **golden age** of motorcycling. Between the two World Wars, the motorbike was more popular than at any other time.

After World War I finished in 1918, soldiers returned home. Many had used motor vehicles for the first time during the war. They now wanted to own one themselves.

To begin with, the army sold off second-hand motorbikes it no longer needed, but it soon ran out. Businessmen realised there was money to be made. Factories that had been producing guns, bullets and tanks during the war were soon producing motorbikes.

By 1919, more than 50 new companies were building motorbikes. By 1921, the number had risen to 100.

Many once-famous manufacturers have now gone out of business.

The Brough Superior was made famous by Lawrence of Arabia.

VINTAGE BIKES

Many famous brands of motorbike disappeared in the 1920s and 1930s. Only bikes built before 1930 can really be called **'vintage'** motorbikes.

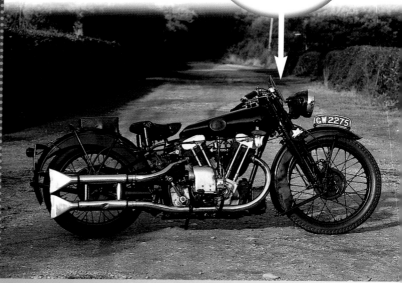

golden age   great period in history
sidecar   small car attached to the side of a motorbike

BIKES FOR EVERYONE

Motorbikes were everywhere in the 1920s. They were used for everyday transport, work and fun. **Sidecars** were built with enough seats for whole families. Butchers and bakers used specially designed motorbikes for making deliveries.

CARS OVERTAKE

By the end of the decade things were changing. Small cars were challenging the motorbike. Cars had become cheap enough for most people.

Before long, many famous motorbike names had disappeared. Sunbeam, Douglas and AJS were among the famous makes that went out of business. By World War II, the golden age of motorcycling was over.

BROUGH SUPERIOR

The Brough Superior was the first great motorbike built for speed. In its day, it was called the Rolls-Royce of motorbikes. It was made between 1924 and 1939 and could go more than 160 km/h (100 mph).

The engine of the Brough Superior.

vintage   old, usually built between 1919 and 1930

11

MILITARY MOTORBIKES

Motorbikes have been used in war for as long as aircraft. About 20,000 motorbikes were used in World War I. By the end of World War I in 1918, Harley-Davidson was selling half the bikes it made to the army.

A bike has many advantages in a war zone. It is:
- small
- cheap to run
- quick
- easy to pack into crates
- easy to drop from an aircraft.

Perhaps the biggest advantage is that a bike keeps going when the road does not. Bikes do many different jobs in a war, from carrying messages to attacking the enemy.

GERMAN BIKES

This BMW R75 bike was commonly used by German forces during World War II. Originally designed for use in the desert, it was good enough to **perform** well in any conditions. The **sidecar** usually had a machine gun built on to it.

A Special Forces trailbike.

military   to do with the armed forces, especially the army

ARMY BIKES TODAY

Today's **military** bikes have to cope with many different conditions. Bikes have been used in desert situations such as the 1991 Gulf War and the 2003 war in Iraq.

Military bikes are built to very high standards. They have to cope with sand clogging up their engines. The bikes run on diesel fuel, so they do not perform as well as petrol engines. The army had to find a way to make bikes run on diesel because all other military vehicles use this fuel.

TECH TALK

In World War II the German army used new tactics to move quickly. Motorbikes meant the army could move and attack very quickly.

FLYING FLEA

The Royal Enfield Flying Flea was a tiny 125 **cc** British bike. It was designed in 1940 for use in World War II. It was light enough to be dropped by parachute and carried by hand.

DESIGN TECHNOLOGY

Modern motorbikes have many different working parts. They are very different from the first motorbikes that appeared about 100 years ago. They are carefully designed and put together. They use the most up-to-date technology.

SIMPLER TIMES

Early motorbikes, such as the Norton Dominator above, were not very complicated. They were not very comfortable or efficient, either. There was no key to start the bike and signals were often given by hand.

LESS GIVES YOU MORE

One of the main differences between a modern motorbike and its older relatives is the number of **integral parts**. This means more things are built all together on modern bikes. They are not built separately, then bolted to one another.

A modern bike with fewer separate parts is lighter and easier to look after.

windshield

bodywork

exhaust

brakes

engine

spoke

　　integral parts　parts of a motorbike built in a single piece, rather than joining several pieces together

NEW TECHNOLOGY

Less weight means more speed. Lightweight metals such as aluminium and titanium are used to build the engine. Many **components** are glued together with super-strong **bonding** materials. This is better than the old way of **welding**, which adds weight to the machine.

The bodywork is made of lightweight plastic, which is getting thinner and stronger all the time. The metal wheels have thinner walls and fewer **spokes**. All these developments help to improve the bike's **performance**.

As years pass by, motorbikes look less and less like the early versions. The thrill and fun of riding on two wheels is still the same.

SHOCK ABSORBERS

Shock absorbers above the wheels have two main parts: a steel spring and a **piston** connected to it. The spring absorbs the bumps as the bike travels. The piston moves inside a tube that is filled with gas, liquid or air.

The suspension system on a motorbike.

spoke metal rod that runs from the centre of a wheel to the outside edge

ENGINE TYPES

There are two sorts of motorbike engine: **two-stroke** and **four-stroke**.

Engines have one or more **pistons**, which move up and down inside **cylinders**. They are powered by a mixture of petrol and air. This mixture is exploded by a spark from the **spark plug**.

A four-stroke engine pushes the piston up and down four times after each spark. A two-stroke pushes twice. The pistons are connected to the **crankshaft**. The up-and-down motion is turned into a circular one. This motion is then **transmitted** to a chain, belt or shaft that turns the back wheel.

A V-Twin engine.

V-TWIN ENGINES

V-Twin engines power many machines. The two cylinders are set at an angle to each other. This makes the V-shape. These engines make a deep, rumbling noise that sounds very powerful. They are used to power Ducatis and Harley-Davidsons.

An in-line four engine.

crankshaft   part of an engine that is joined to the pistons
spark plug   part of an engine that makes an electrical spark

ENGINE NAMES

Engines often get their names from how the cylinders are arranged. Usually, more cylinders mean less engine **vibration** and noise. This makes the ride smoother. There are many different ways that cylinders can be arranged. Each way has advantages and disadvantages.

Most engines have cylinders that stand up. If they lie down, the engine is 'flat'. The Honda Gold Wing is powered by a flat-six. This means that the bike has a six-cylinder engine, with the cylinders lying flat.

The Suzuki RG500 uses a square-four. This engine has four cylinders that stand up in a square. The Yamaha YZF-R1's engine is an in-line-four. The four cylinders stand in a line inside the engine.

BOXER: THE FLAT TWIN

Originally designed in 1912, this classic flat-twin engine has been used by Porsche, Volkswagen and Harley-Davidson. BMW began to use it in 1922 and it became a legend. A modern version of the Boxer is still in use today.

A Boxer flat-twin engine.

transmitted   passed from one place to another
vibration   very rapid shaking

PRODUCTION MOTORBIKES

Building a **production motorbike** is a complicated job. A **production line** has to be set up. All the different parts have to arrive at the production line at the correct time.

Not all the parts of a motorbike are made by the same people. Parts from other factories are delivered to the production line. The bike moves slowly along the line where the **component** parts are added. Every single component is checked and tested before it is ready to use.

It is important to make sure everything runs smoothly. One missing part holds up the whole line. If the production line stops moving, the bike maker loses money.

SAFETY CHECKS

When a bike rolls off the end of a production line it is checked and tested many times. When it has passed every test, it is given a safety certificate. Only then can it be sold.

A production motorbike is made up of parts from many different places.

MOVING ON

As the bike moves **automatically** along the production line, robot mechanics and skilled human technicians do different jobs. Eventually, the completed bike arrives at the end of the line, ready for a test ride.

New motorbikes are packed into crates and sent all over the world to local dealers. People can look at them in the showroom and decide which one to buy.

TOP TECHNOLOGY

The latest technology is used in factories to build a production motorbike. Computer technology and robot mechanics help to put the bikes together very accurately.

Robots and humans work together on modern production lines.

KEVLAR

Gloves are made from leather but the knuckles and wrists are strengthened by a tough material called Kevlar. The body armour areas in jackets, trousers and suits are also made from Kevlar.

PROTECTION

There are no seat belts, bumpers or airbags on a motorbike. Riders must wear special clothing for protection.

HELMETS

The most popular type of helmet is 'full-faced'. It covers the whole head and has a flip-up **visor**. Special slots let air through to stop it steaming up and getting hot. Riders of **vintage** bikes usually wear old-fashioned helmets to match. These are called 'bash hats' or pilot helmets.

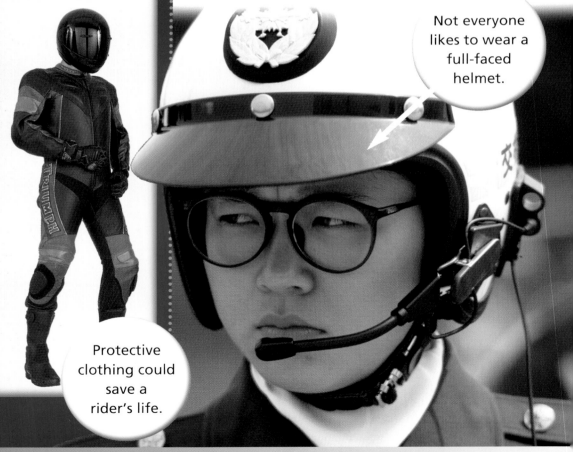

Not everyone likes to wear a full-faced helmet.

Protective clothing could save a rider's life.

armour   protective covering

BODY ARMOUR

Jackets and trousers often have thick pads on the knees, elbows and shoulders. These pads are called body **armour**. They protect the body in an impact (see page 34).

LEATHERS

Leathers can be worn as separate jackets and trousers that are zipped together or as a one-piece racing suit. Motorbike racers normally wear made-to-measure suits. Leathers protect a rider's skin against 'gravel rash'. This is what happens if a rider falls and slides along the road.

BACK PROTECTOR

This is a hard pad worn against the back. It protects the backbone in an accident. Some leathers have a built-in back protector.

FOOTWEAR

Racing boots have thickly protected ankles. The toes and shins are protected by thick plastic. More casual-looking motorbike boots also have this plastic protection sewn inside.

This cutaway shows what is inside a helmet.

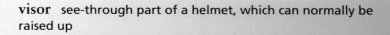

visor see-through part of a helmet, which can normally be raised up

SOME DOS AND DON'TS

Do...
- wear the right protective clothing
- check the bike is safe each time you use it
- concentrate at all times.

Don't...
- overtake or change direction without checking it is safe
- overtake on a bend
- drive too close to other vehicles.

SPECIAL TRAINING

Motorbike riders must be properly trained. On the roads, large trucks and cars can be dangerous to riders.

There are many things to learn, such as:
- the rules of the road
- handling the bike
- safety.

In some countries, such as the UK and Australia, learner riders must attend training courses before they can even start practising on the road. They are taught by professional instructors. The first thing they learn is the layout of the bike and what all the controls do. Then they move on to basic riding, **gear changes** and stopping the bike. Riders must be able to **accelerate** safely, stop quickly and take corners without risk.

Training courses teach new riders how to stay safe.

accelerate   go faster
gear change   changing the speed of an engine

DEVELOPING SKILLS

Next, riders develop their skills on **slalom courses**. These skills will help a rider in slow-moving traffic when they may have to turn sharply and quickly.

Riders learn how to do safe emergency stops and how to control skids. They learn how to spot problems with their machines and put them right.

Once riders are ready, they move on to public roads. To begin with, they usually have an instructor following them. New riders can then use the skills they have learned in real traffic. After several weeks of training, the rider is ready to take a test. If they pass, they are safe and skilful enough to be allowed on the road on their own.

RISKY RIGHT TURNS

New riders spend time practising right turns. Without the proper safety training, these can be very dangerous. A right turn takes the rider across oncoming traffic. The rider could be hit by another vehicle.

Instructors teach new riders to see where the dangers are.

slalom course traffic cones placed in a straight line, a few metres apart; riders must weave in and out between them

MAKING MOTORBIKES

Since the 1960s, Japan has led the way in producing motorbikes. The Japanese have made more motorbikes than everyone else put together. The four big Japanese bike makers are Suzuki, Honda, Kawasaki and Yamaha. They are sometimes called the Big Four.

TECH TALK

Suzuki GSX-R1000 K3: technical data
- Engine size: 988 **cc**
- Engine type: 4-**cylinder**
- Top speed: 280 km/h (175 mph)
- Weight: 168 kg

This was voted International Bike of the Year in 2002.

THE BIG FOUR

The Big Four produce some of the best **performance** bikes on earth. They **accelerate** incredibly quickly. They also have excellent **road-holding**. No one else makes better **production motorbikes**.

The Kawasaki Ninja can reach a top speed of 291 km/h (182 mph).

frame   skeleton of bike, which parts are added to
road-holding   ability of a vehicle to grip the road

THE HONDA FIREBLADE

The Honda Fireblade is a good example of the type of superbike made by the Big Four. This bike led to many great changes in bike design.

The Fireblade was first made in 1992. Many bikes have since copied features of its design. It started a **trend** away from huge engines. The Fireblade had a smaller engine than the superbikes made in the 1980s.

The Fireblade was much lighter than other bikes, so it did not have to be as powerful. It was the first of a new type of superbike. The light **frame** meant a sharper, quicker sports bike. Honda updates the Fireblade year after year, and it is still a best-seller.

A Honda Fireblade.

trend   popular taste at a given time

EUROPEAN BIKES

Japan may have the Big Four, but Europe can produce some fantastic motorbikes of its own. The main European bike makers include BMW, Ducati, Benelli and Triumph.

Europe once had many other excellent motorbike makers – including BSA, Norton, Henderson, Scott, Velocette and Sunbeam. Some of these have disappeared completely. Others only produce a small number of **custom** machines.

European bike makers now concentrate on producing **state-of-the-art** superbikes. A good example is the Benelli Novecento, below. Many experts think it is the best-looking **production motorbike** ever made.

BMW K 1200GT

This BMW K 1200GT is almost as powerful as a top superbike. It also considers the passengers. It has many extras for comfort, such as a CD player, a radio between the rider and passenger, and even a heated seat.

A Benelli Novecento Tornado Tre 900.

custom   special or one-off
radiator   part of an engine's cooling system

BEAUTIFUL BENELLI

The Novecento is unusual because the **radiator** is under the seat. This means the engine can be placed further forward, giving the bike excellent **stability**.

EUROPEAN COMPETITION

European bikes do not sell as well as Japanese bikes. European bikes are well-known throughout the world, though. European bike makers tend to produce specialist bikes, for serious motorcyclists.

European bikes also have a long history and tradition. Triumph and Ducati, for example, have been producing top-class superbikes for decades.

TRIUMPH DAYTONA

The original Triumph Daytona was popular in the 1960s. The modern version has state-of-the-art technology that makes it one of the most famous superbikes on the road today.

A Triumph Daytona 955i.

TECH TALK

Triumph Daytona 955i technical data
- Engine size: 956 **cc**
- Engine type: 3-**cylinders** in-line
- Engine power: 128 **bhp**
- Top speed: 253 km/h (157 mph)
- Weight: 224 kg

stability   not likely to go wrong
state-of-the-art   using the latest technology

AMERICAN BIKES

Cruiser bikes are more about style and looking good than tearing around at high speeds. They are big, powerful and comfortable to ride. The best-known maker of cruisers is the American company Harley-Davidson.

The Harley-Davidson V-Rod looks like an old-fashioned bike. But it goes like a modern one.

HARLEY-DAVIDSON

Harley-Davidson make some of the most easy-to-spot bikes. The Electra Glide Ultra Classic is perhaps the best known of all Harley-Davidson motorbikes. The first version hit the road in 1949. The design has been updated every few years ever since.

V-ROD

The V-Rod's amazing design was inspired by Harley-Davidson's famous drag bikes. This bike appeals to those who love old-fashioned styling. People who prefer more modern-looking motorbikes seem to like it, too.

engineering   use of scientific techniques to improve production methods

ELECTRA GLIDE

The modern Electra Glide has a 1450 **cc** engine. The bike weighs a huge 1840 kg. It comes with a CD player and full sound system. You can even have speakers put into the rider's helmet or talk to a passenger on a radio.

Today's Harley-Davidson cruisers have all the looks and styling of older motorbikes. They also have the **engineering** and technology of today's best bikes.

The Harley-Davidson Electra Glide Ultra Classic has absolutely everything!

The Victory Vegas is a modern version of an old-style cruiser.

29

RACE ACTION

Giacomo Agostini, winner of 122 races.

Road or track racing bikes are designed for speed. The body is **streamlined**, and the tyres are wide and smooth. The engines are ultra-powerful and **accelerate** very quickly.

THE RACING LINE

To win races, riders look for the 'racing line'. This is the route that gets them around the track in the quickest time. Some races, such as the Isle of Man Tourist Trophy (TT) in the UK, are held on real roads. Other races, such as Grand Prix Championship races, are held on special tracks.

TT races on real roads were once part of the World Championship, but now they are separate events. They are more dangerous because they do not have the same safety features that tracks have.

The streamlined shape of a racing bike makes it go faster.

GIACOMO AGOSTINI

Giacomo Agostini won 122 races, more than anyone else. He won eight 500 cc and seven 350 cc World Championships. He also won ten Tourist Trophy titles. In the 1960s and 1970s he earned the nickname 'swivel hips' because of his riding style.

streamlined   shaped to cut through the air easily; this is important for fast bikes

GRAND PRIX

The first Grand Prix took place in 1863. These races have been popular ever since. Hundreds of thousands of people come to watch a single race, with millions more watching on TV. Different classes of Grand Prix are run for different engine sizes. MotoGP, once known as the 500 **cc** Championship, is prized the highest.

A different competition is 'Superbike Racing'. The bikes are very similar to bikes that are used on the road. Only small changes are allowed. This means the races are often close and exciting because the bikes are so similar.

FAMOUS RACERS

Track racers are the most famous motorcyclists. Racers like Barry Sheene, John Surtees, Mike Hailwood and Carl Fogarty are known all over the world.

VALENTINO ROSSI

By the end of the 2003 season, Valentino Rossi had won 59 races and been world champion five times. He is the youngest rider to win all three of the 125 cc, 250 cc and 500 cc/MotoGP world titles.

Valentino Rossi holds the record for the most race points in a season.

RIDING STYLES

Fast bikes need special riding styles and techniques to make them go even faster.

The rider leans forward over the tank. This reduces the **air resistance**. The bike can cut through the air more easily.

Travelling in a straight line is simple. **Gravity** pulls the bike down and it is perfectly balanced. Cornering means that an outward **force** pulls on the bike and rider.

Riders have to be careful. If they lean over too far in a bend, they might just fall off. Top racers have to judge corners correctly every single time. If they do not, the high speeds mean they will certainly fall off.

GEOFF DUKE

Riding styles have changed over the years. Geoff Duke was a huge star in the 1950s. He was World Champion six times. His riding style was very upright. He hardly ever moved his head. This is very different from the knee-down style of today.

Geoff Duke had a very different style from today's riders.

air resistance   slowing-down effect that air has against an object moving into it

LEANING IN

By leaning into bends, the weight of bike and rider acts against the outward force. Leaning over by the correct amount lowers the centre of gravity. With the weight in the correct position, the machine goes quickly around the corner.

Riders also put one knee down towards the track to help this effect. The closer the weight is to the ground, the more **stable** the bike.

Tough pads protect the rider's knees.

Leaning over makes the bike go faster round the corners.

LEANING FOR SAFETY

Leaning over so far in a corner looks spectacular and dangerous. However, riders are moving so fast that if they did not do this they would be in far more danger.

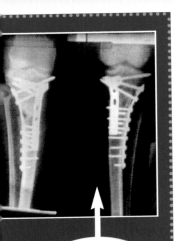

Barry Sheene's legs were shattered in racing accidents. This X-ray shows the metal pins holding his shin bones together.

BARRY SHEENE

Barry Sheene was World 500 **cc** Champion twice in the 1970s. He had two major crashes that almost killed him. His body was rebuilt using many steel plates, bolts and pins. He became known as the 'bionic man of motorsport'.

ACCIDENTS

Bikes can be brilliantly designed and riders highly trained – but accidents will still happen. Mistakes on the road or track still cause injuries.

An accident on a bike is particularly dangerous. There are no seat belts or airbags to protect the rider. There is nothing at all between the rider and the road.

SLIDING

Sliding out is a common cause of accidents. This happens when a rider takes a corner too quickly or the road is slippery. The tyres lose their grip and the bike slides to the outside of the bend. Sliding out happens often on race tracks.

reflective   throws off light

SKIDS

Another common mistake is **accelerating** too quickly. This makes the rear wheel spin in one place. Braking too quickly can also cause a skid. Car drivers can usually stop their cars in a skid or a slide. Skidding or sliding on a bike is a much bigger problem because the rider will probably lose his or her balance and fall off.

BE SEEN AND BE SAFE

Accidents on the road often happen because motorbikes are difficult to see. They are much smaller than other vehicles on the road. If car drivers are not paying careful attention, they could miss a motorcyclist.

Bikers wear **reflective** clothing to make sure they are seen. Many motorbikes can also only be ridden with headlights on.

LEATHERS

Leathers are worn for two reasons. They provide good protection against scrapes and burns if a rider slides off their machine. They also give the rider a **streamlined** shape, which makes the bike go faster.

Bike riders' clothing is the only thing that protects them in a crash.

MOTOCROSS

Motocross is off-road bike racing around specially created tracks. These tracks are full of obstacles, dangers and high-speed sections.

TECHNIQUE

The riders use special techniques when they race. For much of the time the rider does not sit on the seat. Standing up on the bike is called the 'attack position'. This is usually the best way to ride in motocross. Riders must be highly skilled at jumps and landings.

About 40 riders compete in a race. They have to go around the track several times. The race lasts 30 to 40 minutes. Whoever gets around the course quickest is the winner.

Motocross can be very spectacular to watch.

THE BIKES

Motocross riders use special off-road bikes. They do not have a high top speed but their **acceleration** is fantastic.

The bikes have great **suspension** and **shock absorbers**. They need them to cope with all the jumps, bumps and bangs. They also have knobbly tyres to help them grip the dirt. The brakes are sharp and powerful. **Gear changes** are lightning-fast. The engine and **exhaust** are high up. This stops mud getting clogged in them.

Motocross riders need to have great skill.

SAFETY

Because motocross is fast and dangerous, riders wear special clothing with lots of **armour** and padding. The riders must also be fit, strong and have razor-sharp reactions.

TALK THE LANGUAGE

These terms are used to describe parts of a motocross track:

- **Berm:** banked-up corner
- **Drop off:** steep banks, which must be jumped down
- **Tabletop:** jump with a flat top and a ramp at the end
- **Whoops:** bumpy section of track
- **Killer whoops:** very bumpy section of track.

shock absorbers parts of a bike joined to the wheels that allow it to travel over bumps more smoothly

The Baja 500 takes riders across about 800 km (500 miles) of rough country.

ENDURO EVENTS

An Enduro is a long-distance motorbike race. Bikers race over difficult conditions and very rough country. The races are different lengths, but some are up to 1600 km (1000 miles) long. There are also 'Hare and Hounds' races, where riders complete as many laps as possible in a certain amount of time. Time can be very important in an Enduro race. Parts of the race are against the clock. But there are other parts where the challenge is just to finish!

Enduro is a popular sport. Thousands of riders take part in races all over the world. It is a true international sport.

BAJA 500

The Baja 500 is a popular desert Enduro. It starts and finishes in Ensenada, Mexico. The first race was in 1974. There are different races for different sorts of machines.

Temperatures in the Sahara desert often reach 50° Celsius.

ENDURO BIKES

The bikes used in Enduro are very similar to motocross bikes. They do have lights, though, as some parts of an Enduro take place at night. They have to be road legal, because some parts of the race might include normal roads.

PIT-STOPS

At the end of each race stage there are pit-stops where mechanics can check the bikes. The riders carry tents where they sleep overnight.

THE BIG ONE

Paris to Dakar is probably the biggest Enduro race. It begins on Christmas Day (25 December) and lasts into January. The riders must cross the Sahara desert in twenty days. They ride more than 21,000 km (13,000 miles).

AUSTRALIAN SAFARI

The Australian Safari is another very popular Enduro race. Bikers race across extreme desert conditions. The course changes each year, but Darwin to Sydney has been one of the most popular routes.

The Australian Safari takes a different route across Australia each year.

Ice speedway is popular in countries where winters are very cold.

SPEEDWAY

Speedway is bike racing around small oval tracks. It started in the 1920s in Australia. It is very fast, dangerous and exciting. It is a popular sport all over the world.

Speedway bikes are unlike any other bikes you might see on the road. They are stripped down to the basics to keep them lightweight. The 500 **cc** bikes **accelerate** quickly. They can do 0–96 km/h (0–60 mph) in less than 3 seconds, which is as fast as a Formula One racing car. What makes it more dangerous is that the bikes have no brakes or gears to slow them down!

Speedway bikes have no gears or brakes, so riders need a lot of skill.

ICE RACING

Ice racing is a type of speedway that is popular in Scandinavia and Eastern Europe. Riders make the most of the cold weather. The racing is similar to normal speedway, but without the dirt track. Instead, the bikes race on sheets of solid ice.

HOT HEATS

There are four riders in each race, two from each competing team. They ride fifteen **heats**, with each heat being four laps of the track. The track is around 300 to 400 metres long but it is very narrow. The bikes shoot around the dirt track just centimetres away from each other. Any small mistake and all the riders could have an accident.

The tracks are made from loosely packed gravel and dirt. This means the riders slide sideways around the bends, and accelerate along the short straights. The races are short, but very exciting. At the end of the heats, the team with the most points wins.

These spikes dig into the ice for better grip.

TECH TALK

Other types of speedway racing:

- longtrack – much longer tracks, higher speeds, bigger bikes, two gears
- grasstrack – more riders in a race; many different types of race.

DRAG-RACING

Drag-racing is the fastest sport on two wheels. Specially designed bikes are used that are incredibly powerful. They are designed to do one thing: **accelerate** in a straight line as fast as possible.

Drag bikes race in pairs over a track that is about 400 metres long. The race is over in a few seconds as drag bikes reach 320 km/h (200 mph) in under 7 seconds. After the race it takes 800 metres to slow the bike down!

The rider lies flat over the fuel tank. This makes the machine more **streamlined**. It also helps to keep the front wheel down when accelerating.

Without a wheelie bar, this bike would flip over.

DRAG ENGINES

The engine of a drag bike is so powerful it can lift the machine right off the ground. Wheelie bars are fixed to the back of the bike. They stop it flipping over backwards with all the power.

Spinning the back wheel warms up the tyre. A warm tyre grips the track better.

friction   force that slows things down when they move over each other and rub together

DRAG BIKE TYRES

The back tyre of a drag bike is big and wide. The more rubber there is in contact with the track, the better grip the bike will have. Better grip means better acceleration.

Warm tyres grip better than cold ones. Riders warm up tyres before races by doing 'burn-outs'. They rev the engine with the front brake firmly on. The back tyre spins and the **friction** between the tyre and ground warms it up. This produces clouds of thick smoke.

Repeated burn-outs mean the tyres on a drag bike usually last for just six or seven races. As races last for just a few seconds, the lifetime of a tyre may be less than one minute!

A GSX 1588 dragster bike with wheelie bar attached.

TECH TALK

GSX 1588 dragster: technical data

- Engine size: 1588 **cc**
- Engine type: 4-**cylinder** in-line
- Engine power: 375 **bhp**
- Top speed: 296 km/h (185 mph)
- Weight: 211 kg
- Acceleration: 0–100 km/h (60 mph) in 1 second

LAND-SPEED RECORD

There are many different sorts of **land-speed record**. Many riders try to break the land-speed record for motorbikes.

Most record attempts are made at the Bonneville Salt Flats in the USA. This is one of the only places that is long and flat enough for bikes to build up enough speed to break records.

To hold the official world record, two runs must be made inside a certain time. The **average** speed from the two runs is taken. This average speed is the one that ends up in the record books.

Glenn Curtiss also designed and flew some of the earliest aircraft.

GLENN CURTISS

Glenn Curtiss became the fastest man alive in 1907. He rode a V8 bike across a Florida beach at 218 km/h (136 mph). He designed the bike himself, but his record is not officially recognised as it was only over one run.

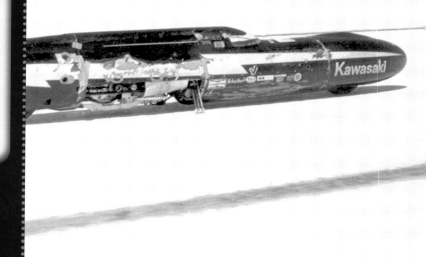

The Lightning Bolt broke the record in 1978.

average   mid-point between two or more numbers

LAND-SPEED RECORD HIGHLIGHTS: TWO WHEELS

Year	Rider	Bike	Average speed
1911	Jake de Rosier (USA)	Indian	136.6 km/h (85.4 mph)
1914	Sidney George (UK)	Indian	149.6 km/h (93.5 mph)
1920	Leslie Parkhurst (USA)	Harley-Davidson	166 km/h (103.8 mph)
1924	Herbert Le Vack (USA)	Brough Superior	190.3 km/h (118.9 mph)
1929	Ernst Henne (Germany)	BMW	215.5 km/h (134.7 mph)
1930	Joseph Wright (UK)	OEC-Temple	241.2 km/h (150.7 mph)
1937	Piero Taruff (Italy)	Gilera Rondine	272.6 km/h (170.4 mph)
1937	Ernst Henne (Germany)	BMW	279 km/h (174.4 mph)
1951	Willem Herz (Germany)	NSU Delphin	288.2 km/h (180.1 mph)
1955	Russell Wright (NZ)	Vincent Black Lightning	296.2 km/h (185.2 mph)
1962	William Johnson (USA)	Triumph Dudek	359.3 km/h (224.6 mph)
1970	Don Vesco (USA)	Yamaha	403.1 km/h (251.9 mph)
1975	Don Vesco (USA)	Yamaha Silver Bird	484.7 km/h (302.9 mph)
1978	Don Vesco (USA)	Kawasaki Lightning Bolt	509.8 km/h (318.6 mph)
1990	Dave Campos (USA)	Harley-Davidson	515.4 km/h (322.1 mph)

Ernst Henne rode a BMW each time he broke the speed record.

ERNST HENNE

Ernst Henne was a brilliant speed rider, and the most successful. He broke the two-wheel land-speed record seven times. His first world record was in 1929, the last in 1937. His final record lasted for fourteen years.

land-speed record fastest speed ever travelled by a particular type of vehicle

SPECIAL MOTORBIKES

Trailbiking is not a competitive sport. You do not earn points or ride against the clock. There is no competition involved. You ride off-road in the country. Trailbiking is a great way to test your riding skills in difficult conditions.

It may not be a competition, but there are important trailbiking rules to follow. The main rule to remember is that bikers cannot simply ride their machines wherever they like. All land belongs to somebody, and bikers must have permission to ride there.

The engine of a trailbike is high off the ground to keep out mud.

Trailbikers ride off-road, through all sorts of country.

RIDING HIGH

Trailbikes are similar to bikes used for motocross. Riders do not want mud to get trapped anywhere. This is why the mudguards, engine and **exhaust** are so high off the ground.

hazard   danger

TAKING CARE

Bikers also need to remember that not everyone in the countryside likes motorbikes being there. It is important not to upset other people using the area. Careless riding could also cause damage to the environment.

The best idea is to join a club. These have regular meetings and help bikers to improve their riding skills. They give advice on the best places to train. They also organise events for members and get permission for the use of land.

Trials-riding courses are difficult and need skilful riding.

TECH TALK

REMEMBER
It is a criminal offence to ride a motorbike:
- in public parks
- on the beach or sand dunes
- over farmland
- on moorland.

Police forces all over the world use motorbikes.

EMERGENCY!

Motorbikes are used all over the world by the **emergency services**. Police forces everywhere use them.

Some police forces use motorbikes because of their speed and power. Big bikes are able to catch up with most vehicles on the road. Another reason for using motorbikes is that they can get around quickly in cities and weave in and out of heavy traffic. A police motorbike can sometimes get somewhere before a police car can. In some countries the police even use small scooters for this purpose.

All police bikes carry radio equipment and basic emergency supplies to help at an accident.

LAW ON TWO WHEELS

Many motorbike makers produce bikes for the police. BMW make more than anyone else. It has produced more than 80,000 police bikes for use all over the world. Kawasaki, Harley-Davidson and Honda also produce machines for the emergency services.

A California Highway Patrol rider.

emergency services   for example, medical services and police

CHiPS

The most famous police motorbikes are ridden by the California Highway Patrol (CHiPs for short). Their main task is to make sure that the law is followed on California's roads.

Until 1997, CHiPs rode Harley-Davidson and Kawasaki machines. Since then they have been changing over to BMWs. There are now almost 1000 BMW police motorbikes operating on California's highways.

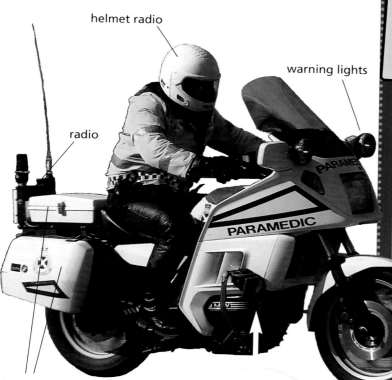

helmet radio

warning lights

radio

emergency equipment

Paramedics' bikes carry equipment for most emergencies.

AMBULANCE ACTION

In some large cities, ambulance staff use motorbikes. They carry most of the same equipment as a four-wheeled ambulance, but can get to the scene of an accident sooner. This is because they can dodge heavy traffic.

EDDIE KIDD

Eddie Kidd made more than 12,000 jumps without breaking a bone. He jumped the Great Wall of China and fourteen double-decker buses. But in 1996 he was badly injured in a crash that ended his career.

Eddie Kidd jumps over a line of buses.

STUNT RIDING

Stunt riding is for people who do not like to ride their machines in the usual way! They attempt amazing tricks and dangerous jumps. It takes great nerve and skill to be a stunt rider.

Stunt riders jump over rows of cars, or across canyons. They ride through flames and along tightropes.

Evel Knievel's 'skycycle'.

Some even jump off their bikes and 'ski' along behind by holding on to the **frame** – at over 160 km/h (100 mph)!

Doing a 'wheelie' is riding just on the back wheel. One stunt rider has done a wheelie at 307 km/h (192 mph). Another rider did a 232-km (145-mile) long wheelie!

EVEL KNIEVEL

Evel Knievel is the world's most famous stunt rider. He made many famous jumps in the 1970s and had several accidents. Knievel joked that he had broken every bone in his body.

In 1974 he tried to jump 500 metres over Snake River Canyon in Idaho, USA. He used a specially designed 'skycycle' powered by rockets, pictured left. Evel made it across the canyon but the skycycle's parachute opened too early. Strong winds blew him back. He floated down and landed just a few feet from the river, where he would probably have drowned.

Evel's son, Robbie, carries on in his father's footsteps. In 1999, he jumped 70 metres over the Grand Canyon.

POLICE STUNTS
Because the police use motorbikes, some have their own display teams. They can do stunts that include jumping over obstacles and riding through fire.

This pyramid involves fifteen policemen.

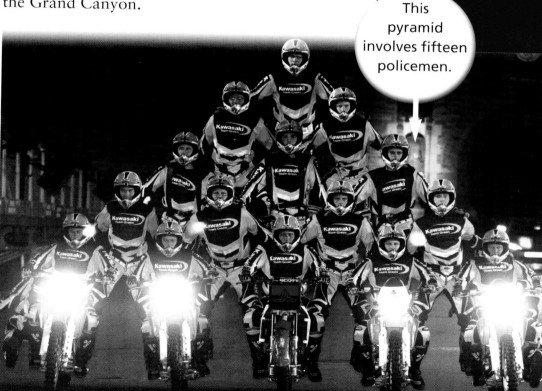

CUSTOM BIKES

A **custom** bike can be many things. It might be a **mass-produced** machine that has been altered in some way. It might be given a paint-job or have a **highly tuned** engine put in. It may even be a one-off special, made from scratch.

Whatever the case, custom bikes are special. They look different from everything else. People who make custom bikes want to own something that no one else has … anywhere!

Custom bikes often have unusual and spectacular paint-jobs. Sometimes even the engine parts are painted. Special paint designs are often done by professional artists and can cost a lot of money.

One of the latest custom-painted helmets by Richard Stevens.

Some people want their bike to be unique – the only one of its kind.

CUSTOMIZED HELMETS

Custom designs can go beyond the machine itself. Some riders even have designs painted on their helmets to match the bike they are riding.

highly tuned   adjusted to make more powerful

SPECIAL TECHNOLOGY

Other custom bikes are more to do with technology than good looks. Some may have special lightweight **frames** that make them super-quick. Others may have special engines or improved **suspension**.

SHOWING OFF

Owners of custom bikes sometimes take them to custom competition shows. These shows are held all over the world. They give the public a chance to see hundreds of amazing machines in the same place. Judges award prizes to the best-looking bikes.

Some custom bikes are very valuable. This is because the parts are specially made. Sometimes parts are even made out of precious materials, such as gold.

TRIKES

Some custom machines even have an extra wheel. They are called trikes. They are quite rare and have to be specially built.

A customized trike.

SCOOTERS

Scooters are small and light. They do not **perform** or handle as well as motorbikes, but they are still great fun to ride.

Like all things, scooters have come in and out of fashion. In the 1960s they were everywhere. Every '**mod**' had to have one, with as many lights and mirrors as possible.

In recent years, the scooter has become popular again, especially in cities. Scooters can get around quickly in traffic jams. They use little fuel, so they are cheap to run.

This Honda Silver Wing scooter looks more like a motorbike.

The BMW C1 has many built-in safety features.

THE HONDA SILVER WING

The Honda Silver Wing is one of the most powerful scooters anywhere. It has many luxury features built in and looks like some of the larger cruising motorbikes.

mod   in the 1960s, one of a group of people who liked the same music and fashion and rode scooters

SCOOTER WITH A ROOF!

The BMW C1, pictured on page 54, is the first scooter to have a roof. The rider sits inside a strong steel **frame**. This means this scooter is safer than most two-wheeled machines. The steel frame protects the rider in an accident.

The C1 has all the advantages of a scooter around a city, but it also has added safety. It even comes with seat belts.

The C1 also has another advantage. It is the only two-wheeled vehicle that keeps the rider dry in the rain!

pictured on page 54

TECH TALK

In many countries you do not have to wear a helmet when riding a scooter. But smart riders always wear a helmet to stay safe.

PEUGEOT SPEEDFIGHT

The Peugeot Speedfight is one of the world's best-selling scooters. It has classic styling but the technology is **state-of-the-art**. It has either a 50 **cc** or 100 cc engine and weighs very little.

The Peugeot Speedfight is a popular modern design.

BIKES OF THE FUTURE

Some future bikes are just too amazing for words. The Tomahawk was an experiment that got lots of publicity. It may even go on sale one day, but there are no plans at present. Only the very rich would be able to buy one. The bike needs four wheels to handle the power of the huge engine. Each pair of wheels is very close together.

A KTM diesel bike.

DIESEL BIKES

Another challenge for designers is to produce a diesel engine that is powerful, but small enough to fit inside a standard frame.

The engine of the Tomahawk is bigger than most Porsche and Ferrari engines. Some military tanks have smaller engines!

The Dodge Tomahawk may become reality one day.

TECH TALK

Dodge Tomahawk concept: technical data

- Engine and size – Viper V10, 8277 **cc**
- Engine power: 500 **bhp**
- Top speed (untested) – 640 km/h (400 mph)
- Weight: 682 kg
- Acceleration: 0–96 km/h (0–60 mph) in 2.5 seconds

carbon-fibre   very hard, strong, light material

NEW MATERIALS

Motorbike design is improving all the time. Bikes are becoming lighter as new materials are used. Aluminium and **carbon-fibre frames** make bikes very light. The less they weigh, the less power they need to move them. This uses up less fuel, which is kinder to the environment.

Computers produce amazing **streamlined** designs. Designers are also working hard to make fuel more efficient. The bikes of the future should be faster, lighter and have better handling.

What they will look like is hard to say. We often imagine that machines in the future will be unlike anything around today. Many bikes of the future could be based on past designs, however. This is called retro-styling.

NEW FUEL

Designers have known for years that petrol engines are not the most efficient. They are working hard to find different power sources for motorbikes. Other possibilities include electricity or hydrogen. Bikers of the future may plug their motorbikes in to recharge rather than go to a petrol station.

This was the first London taxi to be powered by a hydrogen fuel cell.

MOTORBIKE FACTS

Manufacturers with the most Moto GP wins		
Manufacturer	First win	Wins to end 2002
Honda	1961	536
Yamaha	1963	401
MV Agusta	1952	275
Suzuki	1962	153
Aprilia	1987	140
Kawasaki	1969	85
Derbi	1970	81
Kreidler	1962	65
Garelli	1982	51
Gilera	1949	47

The world's longest motorbike jump is 77 m.

There is a river in Arkansas named after Evel Knievel, the motorbike daredevil.

On 2 August, 2003, Billy Baxter rode a Kawasaki Ninja ZX-12R at 164.8 mph along a runway in Wiltshire, England. Billy Baxter is blind.

The world's highest motorbike jump is 7.6 m.

Riders with the most Moto GP Wins		
Rider	Years	Wins
Giacomo Agostini	1965–76	122
Angel Nieto	1969–85	90
Mike Hailwood	1959–67	76
Valentino Rossi	1996–2003	59
Rolf Biland	1975–90	56
Mick Doohan	1990–98	54
Phil Read	1961–75	52
Jim Redman	1961–66	45
Anton Mang	1976–88	42
Carlo Ubbiali	1950–60	39

The world's tallest rideable motorcycle is *Bigtoe*, which has a maximum height of 2.3 m and a top speed of 100 km/h (62 mph). It is powered by a Jaguar V12 engine. The bike cost US $80,000 to build.

The world's longest motorcycle is 7.6 m long, and weighs nearly 2000 kg. The monster machine was designed and built in Western Australia. The bike, which is called *Big Ben*, has a set of training wheels to keep it upright while still. During a test drive, *Big Ben* achieved a speed of 177 km/h (110 mph).

FIND OUT MORE

WEB SITES

BBC SCIENCE
Website packed with games and quizzes to find out about all aspects of science.
bbc.co.uk/science

MOTO GP
Watch videos and read reviews of the fastest superbike races in the world.
motograndprix.com

SPEED RECORD CLUB
Lots of information about the history of the land, water and air speed records, as well as current and future record attempts.
speedrecordclub.com

DUCATI
Find out about this famous company.
ducati.com

BOOKS

Superbikes, Ian Graham (Heinemann Library, 2003)
The Need for Speed: Motorbikes, Philip Raby and Simon Nix (Franklin Watts, 2000)
The World's Fastest Superbikes, Terri Sievert (Capstone Press, 2002)

WORLD WIDE WEB

If you want to find out more about motorbikes, you can search the Internet using keywords like these:

- superbikes + fastest
- 'Barry Sheene'
- motocross
- stunt + motorbikes

Make your own keywords using headings or words from this book. Use the search tips opposite will help you to find the most useful websites.

SEARCH TIPS

There are billions of pages on the Internet so it can be difficult to find exactly what you are looking for. If you just type in 'bike' on a search engine like Google, you will get a list of 15 million web pages. These search skills will help you find useful websites more quickly:

- Use simple keywords, not whole sentences
- Use two to six keywords in a search
- Be precise – only use names of people, places or things
- If you want to find words that go together, put quote marks around them, for example 'world-speed record'
- Use the advanced section of your search engine
- Use the + sign between keywords to find pages with all these words.

WHERE TO SEARCH

SEARCH ENGINE

A search engine looks through the entire web and lists all sites that match the search words. The best matches are at the top of the list, on the first page. Try **bbc.co.uk/search**

SEARCH DIRECTORY

A search directory is like a library of websites. You can search by keyword or subject and browse through the different sites like you look through books on a library shelf. A good example is **yahooligans.com**

GLOSSARY

accelerate go faster

acceleration how quickly something speeds up

air resistance slowing-down effect that air has against an object moving into it

armour protective covering

automatically on its own, without a person working it

average mid-point between two or more numbers

bhp rate at which an engine does work

bonding joining

carbon fibre very hard, strong, light material

cc (cubic centimetres) this number measures the size of an engine's cylinders – a higher number means a larger engine

component single part from something larger

crankshaft part of an engine that is joined to the pistons

cruiser motorbike built for comfort, looks and style rather than performance

custom special or one-off

cylinder tube-shaped part of an engine, where fuel is burned

emergency services for example, medical services and police

engineering use of scientific techniques to improve production methods

exhaust pipe that lets out smoke and fumes

force push or a pull

four-stroke engine where each piston moves up and down four times after each spark of the engine

frame skeleton of the bike, which the other parts are added to

friction force that slows things down when they move over each other and rub together

gear change changing the speed of an engine

golden age great period in history

gravity force that causes objects to fall towards the Earth

hazard danger

heat part of a race

highly tuned adjusted to make more powerful

integral parts parts of a bike built in a single piece, rather than joining several pieces together

land-speed record fastest speed ever travelled by a particular type of vehicle

limited edition when only a small number are built

mass-produced made in large numbers

military to do with the armed forces, especially the army

mod in the 1960s, one of a group of people who liked the same music and fashion and rode scooters

perform / performance how well a bike does things

piston disc or cylinder that moves up and down inside a tube

production line factory system that allows parts to be added to an object as it is moved around

production motorbikes bikes that are built in large numbers to be bought by the public

radiator part of an engine's cooling system

reflective throws off light

reputation being well known for something

road-holding ability of a vehicle to grip the road

shock absorbers parts of a bike joined to the wheels that allow it to travel over bumps more smoothly

sidecar small car attached to the side of a motorbike

slalom course traffic cones placed in a straight line a few metres apart; riders must weave in and out between them

spark plug part of an engine that makes an electrical spark

spoke metal rod that runs from the centre of a wheel to the outside edge

stable / stability not likely to go wrong

state-of-the-art using the latest technology

streamlined shaped to cut easily through the air; this is important for fast bikes

stunt dangerous trick

suspension part of a bike that joins the wheels to the frame; it contains springs that allow the bike to pass over bumps more easily

transmitted passed from one place to another

trend popular taste at a given time

two-stroke engine where each piston moves up and down twice after each spark of the engine

vibration very rapid shaking

vintage old, usually built between 1919 and 1930

visor see-through part of a helmet, which can normally be raised up

welding way of joining metals by melting them together

Raintree would like to thank the following for information used in the book:
The Top Ten of Everything 2004, Dorling Kindersley, 2003.

INDEX